COCKEYED AMERICANA

COCKEYED AMERICANA

A TREASURY OF THE ODD, THE LUDICROUS AND THE DUMB

FOUND, SAVED & SIFTED BY

DICK HYMAN

Foreword by Jimmy Durante. Illustrated by John Devaney. Published by

(Continued on page following)

Cockeyedright notice:

This book has been produced in the United States of America: designed by The Stephen Greene Press, composed by Springfield Printing Corporation, printed and bound by The Book Press. It is published by The Stephen Greene Press, Brattleboro, Vermont 05301.
Library of Congress Catalog Card Number: 72-81526
International Standard Book Number: 0-8289-0170-8

(Continued from preceding page)

THE STEPHEN GREENE PRESS, Brattleboro, Vermont 05301

in the United States of Americana

CONTENTS

FORWARD!

I am walking down Broadway the other day minding my own business when someone slaps me on the neck like a summons server. Blushing like an income tax dodger, I turns around quickly and discover it's none other than my talented friend Dick Hyman. He's one gent that's never too busy to stop and talk to a genius. He grabs me by the arm, shoves me into a taxi, and before I can say gaziggadeegasackeegazobbath, we're at his luxurious office.

He sits me in his Louis XIV chair (the other thirteen guys were out of town) and says, "Jimmy, I'd like you to write a forward—a preface—or an introductory to my new book, 'Cockeyed Americana.'"

"What," I says belligerently, "me—I mean I—write a forward —a preface—an introductory? Are you nuts? You want me to spoil the book? Four hundred words? Why, between Umbriago, Mrs. Calabash, and myself—we don't know that many words. Go get yourself some guy like Bob Considine, Art Buchwald, or Jim Bishop. Those blokes knock a rickety typewriter to pieces with their smart cracks. Me? I'm only a comedian. But okay— let me see the gallery proofs."

Well, I read through all this stuff, see—crackpot laws, wacky wills, daffy divorces, and similar nonsense—and I get me some big belly laughs. So I says to myself, the forward, the preface, and the introductory to this book should consist of four words, namely, COLOSSAL, GIGANTIC, MAGNANIMOUS, and last

1

but not first, AURORA BOREALIS. Four little words that make a sentence—and a sentence that will eventually get me six months.

Believe me, this isn't bad. I once read, or maybe somebody told me, few men make themselves masters of things they write or speak. Don't ask me what it means. But, like the years of research Dick Hyman spent unearthing this collection, it ain't easy, chum, it ain't easy.

It's a lot of fun, this book, and I'm not kidding. This is a big country, America, and we got a lot of loony laws. I heard once that one country is a paradise for women and hell for horses, while another is paradise for horses, hell for women.

Anyway, Dick Hyman travels by dogsled and slow freight to Vermont. He finds an old Vermont law which says a woman can't walk down the street on Sunday unless her husband walks twenty paces behind her with a musket on his shoulder. Some fun, huh?

Then some enterprising legislator gets to work and gets a law passed in Hempstead, New York, which makes it a misdemeanor for a horse to go without head or tail lights when taken for a canter at night.

So, breathing deep of the rich atmosphere of his luxurious office, I stirs in the Louis XIV chair, turns to Hyman and says, "Okay, Mr. Hyman, I'll write a forward—a preface—an introductory to this book."

Jimmy Durante

Here Lies the Body

Epitaphs — last words carved in stone — are found on tombstones in graveyards. Here are a few of my favorites.

In Calvary Cemetery, Chicago:

Dead by the kick of a cow
Well done thou good
And faithful servant.

*　*　*

Near Council Bluffs, Iowa:

Bertha Bright Sparks
May the bright sparks
Upward 'ly.

*　*　*

*A farmer's epitaph
in Wilton, New Hampshire:*

Samuel Brown —
Ripe for the Harvest.

*　*　*

In Middletown Cemetery, Maryland:

I fought a good battle
But I losted.

*　*　*

In New Palestine, Indiana:

GOD'S ANGEL
BAND
WAS NOT
COMPLETE
TILL KATIE
WENT
AND TOOK
HER SEAT.

* * *

In Plymouth, Massachusetts:

If I was so soon to be done for
Why was I ever begun for?

* * *

In Ruidoso, New Mexico:

Here Lies
John Yeast
Pardon Me
For Not Rising

* * *

In Medora, Indiana:

Some have children
Some have none,
Here lies the mother
Of twenty-one.

* * *

In Earlsville, New York:

My Husband
God Knows Why . . .

* * *

HERE LIES THE BODY

In Lee County, Mississippi:

ONCE I WASN'T
THEN I WAS
NOW I AIN'T
AGAIN.

In Pembroke, Massachusetts:

Everything here
is exact to my wishes
because no one eats
there is no washing of dishes.

*   *   *   *   *   *

In Prescott, Massachusetts:

Here lies the body of
      Obadiah Wilkinson
      And his wife, Ruth
Their warfare is accomplished.

*   *   *

*On the stone of a professor
in Elkhart, Indiana:*

School is out
Teacher
Has gone home

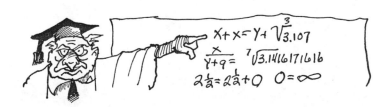

*   *   *

7

HERE LIES THE BODY

In Jacksonville, Florida:

I PROMISE
NEVER TO
MARRY
AGAIN.
     JACK

*   *   *

In Alexandria, Virginia:

Here lies the body of Lizzie Miller
Fast asleep upon her pillow
She was old Henry Miller's wife
And raised the devil all her life.

*   *   *

In Fort Wallace, Kansas:

He tried to make 2 jacks
Beat a pair of aces.

*   *   *

Dizzy Decisions

Ever since the Pilgrims established a permanent settlement on our shores in 1620, judges and justices from the lowest to the highest courts in the land have been handing down decisions on American shenanigans. And some of them are very dizzy indeed . . .

A Tennessee judge ruled that when a widow is anxious to marry and shows the love letters of one suitor to another and boasts about her conquests, such conduct does not evince insanity. If it did, lunatic asylums might have to be very much enlarged.

*   *   *

When the defendant showed up in a Pontiac, Michigan, court without a lawyer, Judge ——— decided to defend him, presented the argument in the man's behalf, then ruled that his impromptu client had lost the case.

*   *   *

11

A municipal judge in Cleveland
said: "If he even threatens you,
pick up the nearest object at hand
and give it to him, but good. And
that's a court order."

* * *

A Salt Lake City court: Prisoners
who are paroled have a right to
take a drink to celebrate their
freedom.

* * *

The arbitrator in a New York
labor dispute ruled that it is not
permissible to fire a waiter
because he is writing a book about
the customers and the restaurant
owner.

* * *

In the Supreme Court of the
United States a unique decision
was handed down in the case of
Egbert vs. Lippman (1881), 104,
U.S. 33, which has been styled as
the "corset case." It was a con-
troversy over the validity of a
patent of a certain type of corset.
Under the patent laws of the time
this case was tried, a patent issued
after two years of public use is
void. The testimony in the case
was to the effect that the inventor
of the corset had let his wife use
one for a number of years before

he applied for a patent. The Court held the patent invalid, stating in the course of its opinion that "the inventor slept on his rights for eleven years."

* * *

A Mississippi district court: When a man has an engagement to take a girl home from a quilting party and he starts to escort her home, but another man interferes and threatens to shoot, the man having the engagement may get his gun and protect himself and the girl, and if necessary kill the other fellow.

* * *

In Nashville, F.S.M., charged with drunken driving, appeared before the judge nine days late, explained why he had missed his first court date: "To tell the truth, Judge, I was drunk."

* * *

In Akron, police testified that they had raided a 9-by-12-foot room, inside found two chairs, a bed, a table, a dresser, three pairs of dice, twelve decks of cards, one bottle of gin and twenty-three men who explained that they had gathered "to discuss current events."

* * *

A Georgia superior court: Those who shoot at their friends for amusement ought to warn them first that it is mere sport.

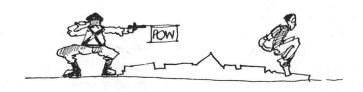

* * *

13

In all solemnity a decision from an Arkansas court reads: "Where the jurors after retiring to consider of their verdict attempted to sing and one of them was unable to carry the bass, it is not ground for a new trial that a man who was not a member of the jury joined them and gave them the proper air."

*   *   *

A Detroit municipal judge ruled that a "friendly kiss" from the boss is assault and battery.

*   *   *

Said a Texas judge in 1911: "It is extremely difficult to draw the line on a drunk. There are various stages, such as quarter drunk, half drunk and dead drunk. There are the stages of being vivacious, foxy, tipsy, and on a

A New York judge declared: "A railway company which negligently throws a passenger from a crowded car on the trestle is held liable for injury to a relative who, in going to his rescue, falls through the trestle."

*   *   *

A New Jersey court ruled that a man who breaks his leg in a three-legged race during a company picnic is not entitled to Workmen's Compensation.

*   *   *

New Jersey State Supreme Court: A woman who does housework for her fiancé cannot collect for it if the man backs out of the marriage.

*   *   *

'high lonesome.' It is about as difficult to determine when a young lady gets to be an old maid as to tell when a man has taken enough alcoholic stimulant to become 'jolly sober' or 'gentlemanly drunk'."

*   *   *

B.M.J. was excused from jury duty in Memphis after he told the defense attorney that he was a professional mind-reader.

* * *

In Fort Worth, C —— R —— was acquitted of drunken driving after he testified that his car had been zigzagging because he was trying to take off a boot that pinched, and that he staggered after his arrest only because the boot was half off his foot.

* * *

Charged with speeding at 64 mph through Milwaukee streets, a motorist was fined fifty dollars despite his excuse: "Another car pushed me."

A New York court held: "There is no such thing as a secret when known by a woman."

* * *   * * *

15

In Laramie, Wyoming, a college student waiting in court to pay a parking fine sat near a group of three men, obediently stood up with them and raised his right hand at the judge's order, was thus sworn in as a new policeman.

*   *   *

An Illinois appellate court: A fleshy woman has a right to ride on a train and to have a valise and parcels, and she is entitled to more time for alighting than might be required for a foot-racer or a greyhound.

*   *   *

L ——— B ———, arrested in Philadelphia after he escaped from the House of Correction, explained that when he had tried to get medical treatment, the prison physician had said, "Get out!"

*   *   *

A Pittsburgh court ruled that it is the railroad's fault if it gives an employee a 20/20 vision rating for a glass eye.

*   *   *

In Knoxville, Tennessee, after their cars collided, W.Z.B. and M.H.H. were freed when they told the judge that the only drinks they had had were a couple of nips while waiting 45 minutes for the police to show up and investigate the accident.

* * *

In Pasadena, when alleged robber J.J.F. was asked by the court if he wanted a lawyer, he replied: "Just give me a machine gun, and I'll get out of here."

* * *

Said a judge in Los Angeles: "No man nor any ordinance promulgated by man can inhibit the habits of rabbits."

* * *

The Kentucky Court of Appeals stated that a wife may pour castor oil in her husband's whiskey because it is a wife's right to try to reform her husband.

* * *

An Omaha municipal court: Husbands who send their wives to court to plead their traffic cases will have to buy their spouses clothes costing the amount of the fines.

* * *

A California court: A drunken man has as good a right to a perfect sidewalk as a sober man, and he needs one a good deal more.

* * *

A court decision in Maine: Everybody is subject to arrest who fishes without a fishing license, including airmen who are undergoing tests for survival in the wilderness.

* * *

An Attorney General in Connecticut ruled that if you are a beaver, you have a legal right to build dams.

* * *

A Somerville, Massachusetts, judge fined a man $15 for drunkenness despite the accused's protest: "It's my new shoes; they hurt so much I couldn't walk straight."

* * *

A New Jersey superior court: A night watchman may be eligible for overtime pay even while asleep on the job.

* * *

DIZZY DECISIONS

A municipal court in Washington, D.C.: A government worker's private hiding place for pencils, pills and mementos is his castle, and no one can tamper with it.

* * *

Charged with rifling the safe of the Farmers' Meat Market in Dallas, R —— S —— explained to detectives why he had carefully padlocked the front door before leaving: "I didn't want some thief to come along and steal all the man's meat."

* * *

When B —— E —— was hauled into a Detroit police court for drinking whiskey, insulting women and eating popcorn in a movie theater, he indignantly protested: "I have never eaten popcorn in my life."

* * *

A court decided that a Binghamton, New York, dentist could not seize and auction the false teeth of a bankrupt woman: the dentures were ruled "a part of a bankrupt's physical person."

* * *

In Bridgeton, New Jersey, an abandoned wife does not have to pay for the clothing her husband was wearing when he left with another woman, a court has ruled. "Do I have to keep on paying for the very shirt and pants in which my husband ran away with another woman?" Mrs. B —— B —— asked. "You do not," the judge replied.

* * *

A North Carolina justice decreed: "A woman of sound mind can deliberately and without justification, murder her husband in cold blood in Tennessee before a dozen witnesses, sign a confession of her guilt, and yet she cannot be legally convicted or even tried for that murder." (*Explanation: A woman in North Carolina fires a bullet from a rifle over the state line into Tennessee and kills her husband. The woman never comes over into Tennessee.*)

* * *

DIZZY DECISIONS

From a case cited in the *New York Law Journal:* "The defendant will be restrained from selling pickles, but not from serving them with meals as a substitute for butter."

A Paterson, New Jersey, municipal court: It is against the law to beat your wife even if she put water in your car's gas tank to keep you from getting to church.

*　*　*

*　*　*

California State Supreme Court: A worker who punched his employer in the nose and received a punch in return is entitled to disability compensation.

Washington State Supreme Court: A child five years old may sue his father for personal injury damages except when inflicted by Dad in the performance of parental duty.

*　*　*

*　*　*

The judge in a Pontiac, Michigan, municipal court ruled that it is unconstitutional, discriminatory and unreasonable for police to ticket ice cream vendors for ringing bells.

*　*　*

DIZZY DECISIONS

The Oklahoma State Supreme Court: Gin is intoxicating.

* * *

A Georgia district court: Love matches exist only in the imagination of novelists.

* * *

An Iowa court ruled that a man has the right to keep his mother-in-law out of his house.

* * *

A court decision in Texas: Ice cream flavored with rum is ice cream and is not in the category of alcoholic beverage.

* * *

A Louisville, Kentucky, court: The dignity of women walking down the street must be preserved and stores must shut off air conditioning systems that blow air through sidewalk gratings and lift up the skirts of the ladies.

* * *

A Minnesota superior court: All young babies look alike.

* * *

A Michigan judge ruled that a woman's hair belongs to her husband.

* * *

A superior court in Ohio: A wife may burn her husband's old fishing or hunting clothes and other "junk" and be wholly within her legal rights.

* * *

The Greenville, New Hampshire, Board of Civil Authority: Wrestling is like Beano and requires a town vote to allow it.

* * *

A Missouri appellate court: It is an inalienable right of the citizen to get drunk.

* * *

The courts of Los Angeles ruled that the weeping of a woman on the witness stand is not misconduct.

* * *

A Florida court ruled that it is not a crime to pick up a girl, because "it is a general tendency of men who see a pretty girl walking along the street to try to get acquainted."

* * *

The Georgia State Supreme Court: It is not necessary for the engineer to blow his whistle for each individual cow on the tracks.

* * *

The Georgia Supreme Court ruled that a man may be fired without notice for taking a sock at the boss. The boss does not have to give the man time to sock him again.

* * *

Said an Arkansas judge: "It is generally supposed, at least among men, that the gentler sex is possessed of almost boundless curiosity."

* * *

The Alabama State Court of Appeals ruled it is illegal to call anyone either a skunk or Adolph Hitler.

* * *

DIZZY DECISIONS

Ruled a municipal judge in New York City: Subway sleepers are human souls whose rights may not be trampled upon and people may snooze away on the subway without being arrested.

* * *

A Vermont superior court: False teeth furnished the wife are necessaries for which the husband is liable if he allows her to wear them.

* * *

A Missouri superior court judge declared: "For a man to swear while trying to button his shirt collar, is not to be regarded as a sympton of softening of the brain."

* * *

An Iowa superior court judge said: "The fact that the husband was not given to much conversation in and about the home may be traceable to the superior qualifications of his better half in that sphere of human activity."

* * *

A decision handed down in Montgomery, Alabama, said in part: "No person shall drive or operate a taxicab who is incapacitated from using both hands and both feet."

* * *

A judge in Wichita decided that you can treat your mother-in-law as badly as you please and your spouse has no grounds for divorce.

* * *

A Maine district court judge observed: "There is nothing certain about a lawsuit except the expense of it."

* * *

DIZZY DECISIONS

A Tennessee judge ruled that a husband under no circumstance or provocation ought to kick in anger his wife when together on the family couch, and even cold feet afford no justification for such conduct.

A New York City magistrate ruled in 1915: "It is disorderly conduct for one man to greet another on the street by placing the end of this thumb against the tip of this nose, at the same time extending and wriggling the fingers of his hand."

* * *   * * *

A recent ruling in Chicago held that a landlord is not permitted to evict a tenant by firing a revolver in his direction.

* * *

A Missouri court: "A man may be absolutely drunk without being dead drunk."

A Wisconsin superior court: It is reckless for a passenger to ride with his body half out of a car window.

* * *   * * *

24

DIZZY DECISIONS

A Marinette, Wisconsin, court: It's not a crime to punch a waiter in the nose if he shows up with the wrong dinner.

*　　*　　*

A New York municipal court: If two women behind you at the movies insist on discussing the probable denouement, you have the right to turn around and blow a Bronx cheer at them.

*　　*　　*

A man who lost his delivery job because he grew a beard is not entitled to reinstatement, a Kansas City arbitration panel decided.

*　　*　　*

A Minnesota circuit court: It is too bad if a golfer loses some teeth by another golfer's drive, but he can't collect damages: golfers should learn to keep out of the way of other golfers' drives.

*　　*　　*

A Michigan judge declared: "For old maids, widows and cautious females to look under the bed for a man, is not evidence of mental deficiency."

*　　*　　*

A Texas judge ruled that a suitor can't hold the cats of the object of his affection for ransom in order to obtain warm responses from her.

*　　*　　*

DIZZY DECISIONS

A ruling from the Director of Public Safety in New Jersey prohibits waitresses from wearing transparent skirts unless their slips are showing.

*   *   *

The judge in a Washington State domestic relations court held that it is very seldom, if ever, that the fondest hopes of wedded bliss are realized by either spouse.

*   *   *

A Georgia court laid this one on the line: "A wife is a wife, and not a husband, as she was formerly."

*   *   *

A Houston, Texas, judge decreed that a man cannot obtain a permit to beat his wife.

*   *   *

Yankee Ingenuity

Take a cross-section census of the United States and you will discover that there is at least one inventor in every hamlet, town and city. Not a day goes by without some inventive soul mailing to the United States Patent Office in Washington his plan of an original idea, contrivance or gadget. Of course, countless patents have contributed enormously to our American way of living. Equally, of course, some have not. Here are a few of the giddy American inventions registered in the Patent Office.

Patent No. 365,672 consists of a device for preventing hens from sitting, and which also operates to induce or influence the hen to lay another clutch of eggs.

The device, an arrangement of spikes, is secured in operative position in a nest so that, when the hen attempts to settle down upon the nest for the purpose of sitting, she will come in contact with the sharp points calculated to make her change her mind. As a result, she gives up the idea of raising a family and lays fresh eggs instead.

*   *   *

Patent No. 292,504 relates to an attachment for locomotives, to be used for frightening horses and cattle off the tracks.

The front end of the locomotive boiler has a forward-projecting tube to which a nozzle is connected by a suitable hinge-joint in such a manner as to be capable of swinging in a horizontal plane. The tube has a stop-cock provided with an arm or handle having at its outer end a crank to which is pivoted an operating rod extending rearwardly to within convenient reach of the engineer.

By means of the rod the stop-cock may be opened, thus permitting water to escape from the boiler through the nozzle with a great degree of force and to a considerable distance so that it may be employed for frightening horses and cattle off the tracks.

* * *

Patent No. 79,063 intends to combine a necktie and watch guard in one neat, convenient, serviceable article, and this is the way it works.

The middle part is passed around the neck and the knot placed. An elastic loop is passed from the front button of the shirt neckband to keep said knot from slipping out of place. The guard ring of the watch may then be attached to the extreme ends of the necktie by a snap-ring, or the watch may be attached permanently to said ends.

Now see what happens. Along comes pickpocket, who lifts the watch while his victim is looking the other way. The necktie comes with it — but only part way: the pickpocket is caught!

* * *

Patent No. 186,962 says, in part, that the applicant has "made a new and useful invention in a 'Pedal Calorificator' or 'Foot Warmer.'

"The invention aims at utilizing wasted heat by a simple contrivance for conveying it to the feet. A light, flexible India-rubber tube, one-fourth to one-half inch or more in caliber, is to be worn between the outer and the inner garments. It is branched and extended from near the wearer's chin to his feet, the upper end of the portion being furnished with a conical or trumpet mouthpiece, within easy reach, and when not in use concealed by the waistcoat. There are two movable hair-pads or cork innersoles to be inserted in the boots or shoes, and to which the branch tubes are either permanently attached or made fast for convenience by loops and buttons under the inside arches of his feet when in place, and so as to discharge obliquely forward to the toes. A suspension neck-collar attached at the upper portion of the tube completes the arrangements, except that a stiff rubber plate may be permanently attached to the tubes at their junction."

* * *

Patent No. 17,192 describes a "deep-sunken boat for trailing and shooting ducks and other water fowl. . . . The hunter may propel the boat toward the game by his feet alone, or, as a simple or cheap arrangement of auxiliary propeller, two paddles or blades may be suspended from the bottom of the boat by rods or chains, and to these rods may be connected a stirrup through which the feet may pass and rest on an arm or projection, on the blades, so that said blades may be worked by the feet."

* * *

And there's a description on file for a device that produces dimples: "Two revolving arms which are pivoted or hinged together after the manner of a pair of compasses, the upper part being connected by a brace. . . . The knob of the arm must be set on the selected spot on the body, the extension put in position, then, while holding the knob with the hand, the braces must be made to revolve on the axis."

It's the Law!

Sandwiched among our country's sound and workable statutes, there are hundreds of cockeyed ordinances that remain to clutter up our law books because the powers that be — from state legislators to town fathers — have not got around to repealing them. Here is a sampling from favorites gleaned over the years. Perhaps a few have by now been rescinded, but the majority are just left to be ignored, and rest in peace.

If you're in Alabama: In Huntsville it is illegal to move your bed without getting a permit from the chief of police. In Tuscumbia it is against the law for more than eight rabbits to reside on the same

block. In Birmingham it is illegal to drive a car while blindfolded. And, since the Alabama husband is accountable for his wife's misbehavior, he has the legal right to chastise her with "a stick no larger than the thumb." Nothing is said about the length of the stick.

* * *

How to behave in Alaska: Fairbanks has an ordinance "to keep moose off the sidewalks." It is illegal to disturb a grizzly bear in order to take its picture. And

there was this notice displayed in the post office at Buckland: "No one shall carry or bring intoxicating liquor to this village. If anyone brings or carries intoxicating liquor, he is to be sent out from this town. Any person shall not tempt any man's wife. A stranger should not stop overnight when the woman is alone. Any persons 'getting together' must have intentions to marry and should a child result of this union the parties must marry."

In Arizona: It is against the law to hunt or shoot camels in the state, and it is unlawful for anyone to ride his horse into a saloon in Prescott.

Football elevens that score against the Arizona Wildcats on their home lot in Tucson face a penalty of a $300 fine or incarceration in the city jail for not less than three months. The pertinent part of the ordinance reads: "It shall be unlawful for any visiting football team or player to carry, convey, tote, kick, throw, pass or otherwise transport or propel any inflated pigskin across the University of Arizona goal line or score a safety within the confines of the City of Tucson, County of Pima, State of Arizona."

*   *   *   *   *   *

IT'S THE LAW!

When you're in Arkansas, remember that: It is illegal to carry a bucket of water down the main street of Clarendon — if the bucket has a hole in it. In Hot Springs it is against the law for anyone to gargle in public. State law forbids a waiter to receive, either directly or indirectly, a tip from any guest or patron. And there is a law that when a train comes to a one-story farmhouse it must blow its whistle once, and when it passes a two-story house it must blow the whistle twice, etc.

* * *

without its master on a leash." In Los Angeles it is illegal to shoot at a hare or jack-rabbit from a trolley car in transit.

* * *

It is against the law when riding a bicycle in Denver, Colorado, to lift your feet higher than the front wheel. Also in Denver, it's the law that you must not step out of an airplane in the air unless there is an emergency. And in Colorado Springs a waiter making an insulting remark to a customer is subject to a fine.

* * *

Then there's California, where: In Pasadena it is against the law for a businessman to be in his office alone with his woman secretary. An ordinance passed by the Belvedere City Council reads: "No dog shall be in a public place

Connecticut state law made it illegal for wrestlers to resort to the use of chairs, bottles, and so forth, to further their cause. No one may fly a kite on the streets of Danbury without a permit from the mayor. An old law prohibited anyone from riding a bicycle more than sixty-five miles an hour.

* * *

In the District of Columbia: It is illegal to catch a fish while on horseback, and it is illegal for a man to engage in a pugilistic encounter with a bull, and it is

against the law to eat while driving a car on the streets of the nation's capital. Owners must remove their boats within five days after they sink along the waterfront. It is against the law for firemen to play cards while on duty. All taxicabs must carry a broom and a shovel.

* * *

Florida school law forbids the transportation of livestock in its school buses. A Winter Garden ordinance states that it is against the law to escape from jail. Police

officers may not gossip while on duty in Key West. In Lakeland anyone owning a rooster has to keep him in a pen or box where he cannot get his head high enough to crow. In Tampa a husband has the right to collect his wife's wages. It is illegal to fall asleep under a hair dryer in Florida. A person cannot buy land that is more than three feet under water.

* * *

IT'S THE LAW!

Rules to remember in Georgia: It is against the law to open an umbrella in front of a mule. In Atlanta it is illegal to have musical horns play "Rock-a-Bye-Baby" on diaper-service laundry trucks. It is against the law to slap a man on the back in Georgia. It is illegal to light a cigarette on any church property in the state. To make faces at school children while they are studying in the classroom is unlawful in Atlanta. In Macon it is against the law for any man to put his arm around a woman without legal excuse or reason. And it is against the law for cats to howl after 9 P.M. in Columbus.

*　　*　　*

In Hawaii: No one may whistle in any drinking establishment, and in Waikiki a man may not be clad only in swimming trunks. All loud

noises are taboo on Sunday, there can be no racing of horses at night, and it is against the law for a person to insert pennies in his ear. A state law says that a barber

shall not lather a customer's chin with a shaving brush; that a barber shall not dust the loose hair from a customer's shoulders with a neck duster; and that a barber or a customer shall not be permitted to sleep in the barber shop.

*　　*　　*

In Illinois: A law in Zion prohibits teaching household pets to smoke cigars; another local ordinance forbids making ugly faces at a fellow citizen. In Chicago a woman may be fined for driving a car with a hat that covers one eye; a knife with a blade longer than two and a half inches must be carried in the open hand, and residents of the city are required to keep fire buckets in their front halls. The sale of ice-cream sodas on Sunday is forbidden by law in Evanston.

*   *   *

An Indiana law forbids anyone to lead young ladies astray while teaching them to roller skate. A Logansport ordinance prohibits wheeling baby carriages on the sidewalks. Taking a bath in the wintertime is prohibited in Clinton. A mustached citizen of Indianapolis may not kiss anyone;

and in the same city it is against the law to quarrel on Sunday.

*   *   *

In Kansas, keep in mind that: Mannequins may not be undressed in Wichita store windows unless curtains shut them away from public view. It is illegal to wash false teeth in public drinking fountains of McLouth. A Kansas City ordinance says that it is against the law to drive a horse without holding the reins. It is unlawful to eat snakes on Sunday anywhere in the state.

*   *   *

According to Kentucky law, women may not appear on the highways in bathing suits unless they carry a club. In Berea any

animal on the streets after dark must prominently display a red tail-light. State law also prohibits

the shooting of clay pigeons during the breeding season; maintains that a person is sober until he cannot hold on to the ground; and requires that anyone operating a still *must* blow a whistle.

* * *

Around Louisiana: In Port Allen hunting rabbits on the main street is prohibited; all pet tigers kept in the town must be caged. Undertakers are prohibited from giving away books of matches in Shreveport. It costs less to bite a person with your natural teeth (simple assault) than with fake teeth (aggravated assault) in New

Orleans. If you complain about the street in front of your home being rough or torn up in Baton Rouge, it's the law that you will be made to fix it yourself.

* * *

State of Maine law makes it illegal for anyone to set a mule on fire; people who walk along the streets with shoelaces untied are subject to a fine; it is unlawful to travel

anywhere on Sunday except for charity or necessity; and according to state law, a wife can sue to recover the money her husband loses in a poker game.

* * *

If you go to Maryland, be warned that: It is against the law to knock a freight train off the tracks. In Hagerstown it is illegal to cross a street by using a rope suspended above it. In Cumberland it is

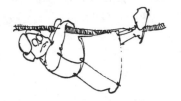

illegal to keep chickens in a hotel room. In Baltimore a man cannot be molested for snoring, even if it annoys his neighbors, so long as the noise is accompanied by slumber; and in the same city, lions may not be taken to the theater. A kiss lasting more than a second is an illegal act in Halethorpe.

* * *

And in Massachusetts: It is against the law to shave while driving an automobile in the Commonwealth. Hissing actors is against the law in Boston. Marblehead regulations state that a three-gallon jug of rum be provided for each fire company responding to an alarm. State law forbids men from going into ladies' hairdressing salons to get waves or hair tinting. In Haverhill

the city council forbids the holding of female wrestling matches on the ground that they undermine the dignity of womanhood. Salem law rules that no person shall smoke any pipe or "segar" in any street, highway, lawn, or public building.

* * *

Whereas in Michigan: State law makes it compulsory for the inmates of the state prison to pay for their own room and board, and also forbids justices of peace to hold court in a barroom. A census of bees is required to be taken each year in Lansing, it is unlawful to hitch a crocodile to a

fire hydrant in Detroit, and serenading your girl-friend is illegal in Kalamazoo.

* * *

IT'S THE LAW!

Be careful in Minnesota, because: It is illegal to display both men's and women's undergarments on the same clothesline. An old law makes it illegal to wipe dishes in Minneapolis.

*   *   *

In Mississippi: It is against the law to play the "Missouri Waltz" on the piano at any hour of the broadcast day. In Natchez, it is

unlawful for elephants to drink beer. It is illegal to shave in the center of Main Street in Tylertown. Merchants in Clara may not reveal to others which of their customers owe them money, or how much. The town of Star has a law prohibiting anyone from ridiculing the public architecture.

*   *   *

If you're from Missouri you know that: No automobile shall be driven on the streets of Trenton after sundown. Saco forbids any person to wear a hat which may frighten "timid persons, children, or animals." It is against the law to ride an ox on Jefferson City's streets in a violent or furious manner. It is illegal in St. Louis to sit on a curb and drink beer out of a bucket. In Osceola bicyclists must politely request permission of all drivers of horse-drawn vehicles before passing them along the road.

*   *   *

When in Montana: If you receive letters from an old girl-friend, you are protected by law from the wrath of your wife, for it is a felony for her to open your letters or telegrams. In Helena it is illegal

to tie your horse to a fireplug, or to indulge in unrestrained giggling on the streets. A fan dancer must wear a costume weighing at least 3 pounds, 2 ounces in a place where liquor is sold, according to state law.

And out in Nebraska: Barbers in Waterloo are forbidden to eat onions between 7 A.M. and 7 P.M. Halsey law states that the town constable shall at all times remember his manners. In Omaha it is illegal to sneeze or burp during church services. It is illegal for burglars to come in or go out the front door in Lincoln. State law says that a woman may use profane language before a man but a man may not use profane language before a woman.

    *   *   *   *   *   *

In Nevada: A teacher must solemnly swear that he or she has never taken part in a duel, either as a principal or as a second, before being allowed to teach in the state. In Nyala no man shall stand treat at a bar for more than three persons besides himself at one time; and in Elko no one may walk on the street wearing a mask.

IT'S THE LAW!

New Hampshire state law holds that, when two motor vehicles meet at a highway intersection, each shall come to a full stop and neither shall proceed until the other has gone. It is against the law to pawn the clothes off your back. In Neligh it is against the law to sell doughnut holes.

*　*　*

*　*　*

Down New Mexico way: It is unlawful for either a man or a woman to go unshaven in Carrizozo. In Dunlap it is illegal to tear up a marriage license. In Albuquerque you must check your shooting irons at the police station within thirty minutes of your arrival. In Quemado any newspaper can be fined if it misspells your name.

According to New Jersey law, any person walking in his sleep is just as responsible for his actions as a person who is wide awake; a person who frowns on a policeman is subject to arrest; and it is against the law to slurp your soup. And it is unlawful to smoke a cigarette in the kitchen of your home in Atlantic City.

*　*　*

And New York: In Rochester it is unlawful for youngsters to collect cigar stumps. Donkeys are not allowed to sleep in bathtubs in Brooklyn. In New York City it is against the law to carry a skeleton into a tenement house. It is against the law to sit on newspapers on the beach on Coney Island.

* * *

Elephants may not be used to plow cotton fields in North Carolina; a state law makes it illegal to sing out of tune; and twin beds must be two feet or more apart in all hotels. In Charlotte it is the law that there must be at least sixteen yards of cloth around the body of a woman when she is on the streets.

* * *

Take care in Ohio, because: If you ignore an orator on Decoration Day to such an extent as to play croquet or pitch horseshoes within one mile of the speaker's stand, you can be fined $25; also it is illegal to fish for whales in any stream, river, or lake on Sunday. A Dayton ordinance forbids the feeding of a cow or hog on any of the sidewalks within the city limits. In Cleveland it is unlawful for two men to drink out of the same whisky bottle and get drunk at the same time.

* * *

Oklahoma law says that: It is illegal to yell on the public streets. A woman must have a license to curl or otherwise dress her own hair. An ordinance requires every public eating house in Bristow to serve each customer or patron one peanut in the shell with each glass of water. In Yukon it is against the law for a patient to pull a dentist's tooth. In Oklahoma City it's against the law to toss a snowball.

*   *   *

In Oregon: Monmouth law decrees that a young woman may not enter an automobile with a young man unless accompanied by a chaperon. It is illegal to wear roller skates in public rest rooms in Portland, nor may anyone shake a feather duster in another person's face. In Klamath Falls it is against the law to kick the heads of snakes. In Baker it is illegal to speak to a female against her will. In Burns the law forbids cowboys to ride their horses into saloons unless they pay admission.

*   *   *

have a corresponding tooth pulled by the village blacksmith or pay a fine; in Central Falls it is against the law to pour pickle juice on the streetcar tracks; and in Peace Dale it is unlawful to give a girl a cigarette. Rhode Island prison inmates have a legal right to change their underwear once a week. Drugstores in Providence may sell toothpaste but not tooth-brushes on Sunday.

*   *   *

Pennsylvania law says that all restaurants must be equipped with stretchers and wheelchairs. Throwing hoop skirts on the streets is a crime in Philadelphia. A Morrisville ordinance makes it unlawful for men to shave or women to wear cosmetics if they do not have a permit. A Dupont law required that intoxicated persons down a sizable dose of castor oil. It is against the law for a baby sitter to clean out her employer's icebox in Altoona. In Lawrenceville it is illegal to walk down the streets after sundown without carrying a lighted candle.

*   *   *

On the other hand, in Rhode Island: An ordinance in South Foster provides that a dentist who extracts the wrong tooth must

A South Carolina statute requires every law-abiding man to take his gun to church on Sunday. In Spartanburg, it is illegal to eat watermelon in the Magnolia Street cemetery. A law prohibits hip pockets because they furnish a convenient place for pint bottles. In Anderson it is illegal to curl up on the railroad tracks for a nap.

48

IT'S THE LAW!

State law forbids a butcher to sit on a jury when a man is being tried for murder.

* * *

In South Dakota it is illegal to sleep in a cheese factory, women over 50 years of age may not speak to married men over 20 on the sidewalks and streets, and it is against the law to buy a quart of ice cream on Sunday. In Aberdeen it is against the law not to give fair warning before driving into town with a "horseless carriage." State law says that it is illegal for a theater manager to show a "whodunit," or any picture with scenes illustrating illicit love, infidelity, murder, or the striking of an officer of the law.

* * *

An old law in Tennessee says that a person must pay his state poll taxes in squirrel, crow, or wolf scalps. In Knoxville it is against

the law to lasso a fish. It is unlawful in Kingsport to sell soft drinks on Sunday during church services. In Bristol it is illegal for women to fix their stockings on the streets.

* * *

IT'S THE LAW!

And in Texas: Ladies depicted on calendars hanging in public saloons must be decently clad. In Dallas it is unlawful for any person to carry or display sandwich signs derogatory to the business or person of another. No automobiles may come within three miles of the city limits of Silverton. In Amarillo it is against the law to take a bath on the main street during banking hours. And a man served a term in the Texas State Penitentiary for the offense of worthlessness.

*   *   *

Women in Utah must remember that a state law forbids them to wear heels more than 1 1/2 inches high. Local pharmacists in Trout Creek may not sell gunpowder as a headache cure. In Provo it is against the law to strike a match, and in Salt Lake City it is a misdemeanor to give away a fish on Sunday or a legal holiday.

*   *   *

Vermont state law declares that a woman cannot walk down the street on Sunday unless her husband walks twenty paces behind her with a musket on his shoulder. A person may not jump out of an airplane without the express permission of the Vermont Aeronautics Commission. In Vermont it is against the law for a person who has arrived at the age of discretion to profanely curse and swear. A town regulation in Morrisville requires that anyone desirous of taking a bath must first secure a permit from the board of selectmen.

*   *   *

Meanwhile, in Virginia: State law forbids bathtubs in the house: tubs must be kept in the yard. It is illegal to tickle a girl in Norton; and it is against the law for hens to lay eggs before 8 A.M. and after 4 P.M. in Norfolk. It is

In Washington: A Seattle ordinance requires every householder to set at least two rat traps each day. Men are forbidden by law to blow their noses outdoors in Leahy lest they frighten a horse.

* * *

Wisconsin is horse-conscious too: A Milwaukee regulation decrees that no automobile may be parked over two hours unless hitched to a horse. State law makes it illegal for any spectator

unlawful for a girl to attend a public dance in Norfolk without wearing a corset; the law further states that, if a girl checks her corset, the dance hall shall have its license revoked.

* * *

to make any remarks during a prize fight. In Fox Point it is illegal for dogs to travel in groups larger than two. In St. Croix an ordinance forbids ladies to be seen on the street in red clothing.

*   *   *

And finally, in Wyoming: Women are required to stand five feet away from bars when drinking in public anywhere in the state. It is illegal to shoot buffalo from the barracks windows in Fort Warren. In Casper it is against the law to loan city water to a neighbor except for drinking purposes.

*   *   *

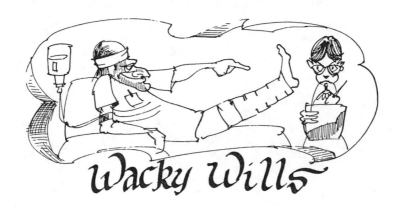

Wacky Wills

The last will and testament of a person is usually binding, no matter how oddly phrased or far-fetched it may read, so long as it meets the provisions of the probate court. Last wills and testaments have been written on everything imaginable, including prescription blanks, the back of bridge scores, visiting cards, dance programs, the bark of a tree and even tattooed on the human skin. All have been admitted to probate.

Wills have exposed the whole gamut of human emotions, including humor. The following odd-ball requests and bequests were duly carried out according to probate records.

One man disposed of $6 million with a will scrawled on a hospital chart.

Another did not have a chart handy but one of his nurses lifted her dress and he wrote it on her slip. A second nurse witnessed his will. Most of his big estate went to his grand-niece but each nurse got $10,000 for "devotion to duty."

An alcoholic who died following a bad case of delirium tremens left $5,000 each to "the nurse who removed a pink monkey from the foot of my bed, and to the cook at the hospital who removed snakes from my broth."

* * *

The will of a certain wealthy, and dyspeptic, banker read in part: "To my wife, I leave her lover and the knowledge I wasn't the fool she thought I was. To my son I leave the pleasure of earning a living. For 25 years he thought the pleasure was mine. He was mistaken. To my daughter I leave $100,000. She will need it. The only good piece of

business her husband ever did was to marry her. To my valet I leave the clothes he has been stealing from me regularly for the past 10 years, also the fur coat he wore last winter while I was in Palm Beach. To my chauffeur I leave my cars. He almost ruined them and I want him to have the satisfaction of finishing the job. To my partner I leave the suggestion that he take some other clever man in with him at once if he expects to do any profitable business."

* * *

Altogether unique was the whim of a rich old bachelor, who, having endured much from "attempts made by my family to put me under the yoke of matrimony," conceived and nursed such an antipathy to the

fair sex as to impose upon his executors the duty of carrying out what is probably the most ungallant provision ever contained in a will. The words are as follows: "I beg that my executors will see that I am buried where there is no woman interred, either to the right or left of me. Should this not be practical in the ordinary course of things, I direct that they purchase three graves, and bury me in the middle one of the three, leaving the two others unoccupied."

*   *   *

A New Yorker left this will on his death in 1880:

"I bequeath all my fortune to my nephews and nieces, seven in number.

"They are to share it equally, and on no account to go to law about it, on pain of forfeiting their respective shares.

"I own seventy-one pairs of trousers, and I strictly enjoin my executors to hold a public sale at which these shall be sold to the highest bidder, and the proceeds distributed to the poor of the city.

"I desire that these garments shall in no way be examined or meddled with, but disposed of as they are found at the time of my death; and no one purchaser is to buy more than one pair."

As the testator had always been more or less eccentric in his ways, no one was much surprised at these singular clauses, which were religiously observed. The sale was held, and the seventy-one pairs of trousers were sold to seventy-one different purchasers. One of these, in examining the pockets, discovered a packet of some sort, closely sewn up. He lost no time in cutting the thread, and was not a little surprised to find a bundle of banknotes amounting to a thousand dollars. The news soon spread, and each of the others found himself possessed of a similar amount.

*   *   *

In 1879 a man died who willed that his friends were to take turns rolling a barrel of beer after his hearse and consume it on his grave. Another old will provided that a new cooking recipe should be pasted on the testator's tomb each day due to the fact that his wife had been such a poor cook.

*   *   *

An old bachelor left all his property to three ladies to whom he had proposed marriage and who had refused. "By their refusal," he stated, "I owe all my earthly happiness." One disillusioned lawyer left $10,000 to a local madhouse, declaring it was simply an act of restitution to his clients. A Nashville, Tennessee, businessman willed to his sister "a round-trip ticket to my funeral."

*   *   *

WACKY WILLS

On his death in 1959, movie star Wayne Morris willed that $100 be spent at his funeral for "booze and canapés," and then added: "Make it $300, because I don't want my friends to go away sober or serious."

M ——— H ——— willed $150,000 and an opera that he composed to the world-famed Metropolitan Opera in New York. But there was a catch to the bequest: if they wanted the money they had to take the opera. They took neither.

* * *

A bit player named Conrad Cantzen, who had long been out of work and lived on the bounty of friends, died in 1945. The Actors Fund paid his final hospital bill and financed his funeral. In his small, bare room a will was found which stipulated that, because he had often walked the rounds for miles on thin-soled and battered shoes, he was setting up a Shoe Fund for actors who couldn't afford them. The fund was over $225,000. And actors who need shoes today, still draw on it.

* * *

An enthusiastic card player left to certain of his card-playing friends a legacy of a certain amount on condition that, after placing a deck of cards inside his coffin, they should carry him to the grave, stopping on the way to have a drink at a certain tavern where he had passed "so many agreeable evenings."

WACKY WILLS

Dour wills are not a modern invention. Back in the eighteenth century a crabbed husband was the author of the following:

"Since I have had the misfortune of having had to wife one Martha M——, who, since our marriage, has tormented me in a thousand ways; and since not content with showing her contempt for my advice, she has done everything that lay in her power to render my life a burden to me; so that Heaven seems only to have sent her into the world for the purpose of getting me out of it sooner; and since the strength of Samson, the genius of Homer, the prudence of Augustus, the skill of Pyrrhus, the patience of Job, the subtlety of Hannibal, the vigilance of Horatio, would not suffice to tame the perversity of her character; weighing carefully and attentively all these considerations, I have bequeathed and do bequeath, to Martha M——, my wife, one shilling."

*   *   *

A maiden lady over fifty years of age, with a strong aversion to all theatrical amusements, was scandalized by being put down for a legacy in the will of a facetious friend, who attached the condition that within six months of the testator's death the legatee must obtain an engagement at a theater and perform there for one whole week.

*   *   *

A lady in Binghamton, New York, left her husband a new wife. Her will ordered that they be married five days after her funeral. The bride was the lady's daughter from a previous marriage.

*   *   *

A spinster in New York desired that all the money she should be possessed of, might be employed in building a church in her native city, but stipulated that her remains should be mixed up in the mortar used for fixing the first stone.

A young lady in Kentucky exhibited a depth of sentiment rarely equaled, when she directed in her will that tobacco should be planted over her grave, so that the weed, nourished by her dust, might be smoked by her bereaved lovers.

*   *   *

A rich man left legacies to all his servants except his steward, to whom he gave nothing, on the plea that, "having been in my service in that capacity twenty years I have too high an opinion of his shrewdness to suppose he has not sufficiently enriched himself."

*   *   *

Hobby Lobby

All of us have some form of hobby. Maybe it is collecting stamps, match covers, coins, photographs, or old letters; perhaps it has to do with something else. Here are some pastimes and pursuits of other Americans.

A physician and surgeon from Three Rivers, Michigan, perfected a method of painlessly extracting teeth. At times he extracted 400 teeth in one day. He had over a bushel of teeth in his barn, and made three signs out of teeth as a curiosity.

* * *

J ——— L ——— of Los Angeles collects jobs. He held seven jobs at one time; never has been fired; and claims the greatest variety of jobs in the world.

* * *

D ——— F ——— of Boston reads the telephone directory for relaxation.

* * *

HOBBY LOBBY

Racing baby turtles is the hobby of a man from West Newton, Massachusetts. He has a circular track on a bridge table with an automatic starting gate. It's built like a regular race track. It takes about one hour to get a turtle into racing condition, he reports.

* * *

When Mrs. M ——— D ——— of Wilmington, Ohio, finished reading the Bible upside down, she then read it backward upside down commencing with the last word.

* * *

A.D.M. of Chicago enjoys freezing herself in ice. She says it proves that the body can stand the cold if the person has a strong will power.

* * *

There is a fellow in St. Louis who likes to approach people and ask them if he looks like a bum.

* * *

A man in South Dakota lifts weights of 100 pounds or more with his ears. A man in Greensboro, North Carolina, collects fleas from the neighbors' dogs and cats and sends them to a biology supply company after putting them in alcohol; he gets one penny for each flea.

* * *

J.H.D. of St. Paul, Minnesota, collects locks of hair from every girl he kisses, pastes them on paper with the date, place, and name, and also notes his impressions. Has over 300 locks — all colors.

* * *

J ——— C ——— of Vandalia, Illinois, blows up rubber inner tubes until they burst, a feat which takes 1 minute and 45 seconds to accomplish.

* * *

F ——— V ——— of Philadelphia camouflages black eyes.

* * *

New York boasts a hobbyist who has collected more than 150 systems of playing the horses. He bought a system that cost the original purchaser $100 — he got it in a secondhand shop for a nickel.

* * *

J—— T—— of Burnell, Nebraska, makes a hobby of eating. He has eaten seventy-seven pancakes in eight minutes; three quarts of ice cream at one sitting. He weighs only one hundred and forty-five pounds and is five feet seven inches tall.

* * *

A lady residing in Charleston, West Virginia, makes a practice of keeping straight pins in her mouth at all times. She likes the taste. If they turn sour, she spits them out.

* * *

S—— G—— of Chester, Virginia, has a hobby of bees. He has over one hundred hives. He fills his hat full of bees and puts it on his head covering his face with his pet bees; even places them in his mouth. Yet he has never been stung.

* * *

M—— S—— of New York City collects cigar butts and thus tells the character of the smoker. He has a large collection of cigars smoked by such famous people as James A. Farley and Al Smith.

* * *

F—— H—— of Atlanta, Georgia, likes to drive nails (twelve- to twenty-penny in size) through a board from one to two inches thick with his hand in one single stroke.

* * *

70

HOBBY LOBBY

A lady from Eugene, Oregon, has a hobby of raising snails. A young girl from Chicago, saves chewed chewing gum: her stamp collection began getting dull so she started collecting the gum that she had chewed.

* * *

S—— C—— of Shamokin, Pennsylvania, writes seven different ways: both hands, both elbows, both feet and mouth; backwards, and upside down.

* * *

The hobby of C—— E—— of Memphis, Tennessee, is sleeping on buses. So far, she has traveled forty thousand miles on them and slept thirty-five thousand of the miles.

* * *

Daffy Divorces

The time-worn adage that "Truth is stranger than fiction" gains broad support in the divorce courts of our nation, where human antics provide not only pathos and humor but a generous measure of slapstick.

Mrs. L ——— N ——— told a judge in Detroit that her husband spent all his time reading the dictionary while she worked, and on her return home each day forced her to learn ten new words and answer an oral quiz on them.

In Los Angeles, V —— C —— complained to the court that his wife had moved her mother, her brother and her daughter by a previous marriage into his six-room house, then started going out nights with other men.

*   *   *   *   *   *

The father of eleven children said he didn't mind so much living in the barn with the cows for two weeks while his mother-in-law visited; but what finally drove him into the divorce court was the birth of two calves, which crowded him out of the stable and forced him to sleep with the chickens in the hen house.

*   *   *

DAFFY DIVORCES

In Cleveland, Mrs. H——— T——— won a divorce after testifying that when she was about to have a baby, her husband dropped her off at the hospital, then hurried around the corner to have a date with a nurse. Another woman was granted a divorce when she told the judge that since their marriage her husband had spoken to her but three times. She was awarded custody of their three children.

*   *   *

A Wichita, Kansas, judge ruled that you can treat your mother-in-law as badly as you please and your spouse has no grounds for divorce.

*   *   *

In Hollywood, R—— M—— got a decree after she charged her husband left her alone with company and went off to his room to play with his electric trains.

*   *   *

In Los Angeles, Mrs. H——— L——— said during divorce proceedings that her husband phoned from the office one night, told her he would be working late and had not yet come home — after two years. Also in Los Angeles, Mrs. S——— L———, suing for a divorce, said her husband would show off before friends by presenting her with a $1,000 check, then tear it up after the guests had gone.

*   *   *

DAFFY DIVORCES

The judge granted a divorce to a Spokane, Washington, woman who said her husband used a hatchet on the Christmas turkey — not to kill it but to carve it. She said it was a reflection on her cooking.

*   *   *

In Portland, Maine, E ——— E ———, contesting her husband's divorce, testified that after a family spat he "broke my teeth and my nose, tore my ear, broke my arm and some ribs, but outside of that he's an awful good man and there's no one in the world I love more."

*   *   *

In Cincinnati, L ——— H ——— accused his wife at a divorce hearing of placing gummed stickers around the house reading, "Be sure to put dirty hands on the wallpaper; be sure to slop up the mirror; be sure to mess this up; might as well put the garbage in the living room."

*   *   *

In Miami, Mrs. A —— L —— filed for a divorce on the grounds that her husband tried to exchange her and their eight-year-old daughter and their eleven-year-old twins as trade-ins for a new car.

*   *   *

DAFFY DIVORCES

A divorce was granted a Des Moines woman who said her husband never gave her any Christmas presents because he still believed Santa Claus would provide. A North Dakota wife divorced her husband because he refused to build a bathroom in her new home: she testified he thought sanitary facilities were something newfangled and wouldn't last.

* * *

In Cleveland, W —— O —— got a divorce after testifying that his second wife, H ———, insisted that he attend mind-reading seances and then informed him he must obey her orders since she was getting instructions from his deceased first wife.

* * *

A Trenton, New Jersey, wife charged that her husband beat her whenever the New York Yankees lost a game. And in

Chicago a woman cited among her husband's "acts of cruelty" that he painted spectacles and a mustache on her wedding picture.

* * *

As fond as he was of animals, a husband brought suit because he simply could not put up with his wife's habit of letting a pet monkey sleep in the bed. But the judge took an unexpected view when he granted the wife the divorce with alimony because the husband did not have gumption to toss the monkey out of the bed.

* * *

78

In Albuquerque, New Mexico, a soldier got a divorce after declaring in a sworn statement from Japan that he joined the Army to get away from a hypercritical wife: "I was blamed for dust storms, the heat, the cold and all the natural phenomena indigenous to Albuquerque, and I just couldn't take it any more."

* * *

When a wife kicks a husband out of the house, she is the deserter, not the husband. So ruled a Domestic Relations judge in Providence, Rhode Island, when he granted a divorce to a man who was chased from his house four years earlier.

* * *

Another harried husband cited a long list of cruelties practiced by his wife. She threatened him with a knife and beat up his mother. But what hurt him most, he said, was when she stole his five prize rabbits.

* * *

One husband told the judge that his wife didn't want him to make a living. He claimed that early in the morning she let the air out of his tires so he would have to push the car a block to the nearest filling station.

In Hackensack, New Jersey, the defendant hotly denied his wife's charges that he had mistreated her, told the judge: "I never laid a hand on my wife since I broke her arm on January fifth, 1950."

* * *

A California husband told the judge his reason for wanting a divorce was that his wife hired a private detective to keep tabs on him and then made him pay the bill.

* * *

A wife may be granted a divorce in Georgia if her husband is in the military service of the United States, according to a law of 1864.

* * *

* * *

A 90-year-old man in Indianapolis divorced his wife, 65, who left him after only one day of marriage. He commented to the judge, "I guess she was too young for me."

* * *

DAFFY DIVORCES

A preacher sued his wife because she made faces at him during his sermons and also, on occasion, went to sleep and snored during his services.

*   *   *

Mrs. M —— N —— of Detroit got a divorce when she told the judge she had to work to support herself because her husband lavished so much money and affection on his 10,000 pet worms.

*   *   *

In Tulsa, Oklahoma, a judge considered the custody of a car belonging to a couple awaiting their divorce — finally awarded it to the husband for business and to the wife for weekend shopping.

*   *   *

A Los Angeles court decreed that a husband may visit his divorced wife's cocker spaniel occasionally and take it for walks.

*   *   *

In Albuquerque, Mrs. J —— G —— asked the district court to set aside her divorce because (a) her husband had not told her he filed for it, (b) she signed the divorce writ thinking she was signing a wife-beating complaint, and (c) she and her former husband had since become reconciled and had had three children.

*   *   *

In Detroit a philandering husband told the judge "there are too many good-looking women around" — and got a rider to his divorce restraining him from marrying for two years.

*   *   *

In Chicago, a woman whose husband manufactured fly-swatters said he continually used them to swat her. And in Memphis, a woman sued for divorce asking custody of the family phone. Another woman in Des Moines complained that her husband had been in bed for seven years, although in perfect health, and was still there.

* * *

In Cleveland, Mrs. N—— S—— told a divorce court that when she asked her husband to explain a package of love letters from a nightclub entertainer, he laughed, retorted, "This is a modernistic world," then broke a mirror over her head.

* * *

In Cincinnati, Mrs. R—— P—— got a divorce after telling the judge that "the only thing my husband bought for me in all our married life was a pair of shoes—and they hurt."

* * *

A Passaic, New Jersey, wife sued her husband for divorce on the grounds that he objected to her daily hot showers, and complained to her: "You should have married a millionaire or somebody who owns a gas company."

* * *

Mrs. K—— T—— told the divorce court that, among other things, her husband beat her once a month, usually with a bed slat, and opened all the windows in the midwinter when she tried to take a bath.

* * *

DAFFY DIVORCES

A Detroit wife got a divorce after she complained to the judge that her husband inspected the garbage every night before she threw it out and bawled her out if he found the potato peelings too thick.

* * *

A Milwaukee resident who was a veteran of five years in the Army, filed suit for divorce, claiming he was "shocked" by his wife's profane conversation.

* * *

In Los Angeles, suing for divorce, Mrs. R—— H—— complained that her husband told her he should have married his brown-eyed childhood sweetheart and often played a recording of "Beautiful Brown Eyes."

* * *

A husband brought suit in domestic relations court, complaining that the never-ending search for his wife's lost belongings amounted to extreme mental and physical cruelty. "Although I am good at finding them, it is particularly trying," he testified, "when I must hunt for a lost black glove in a theater or under a restaurant table. It makes me feel like a bloodhound sniffing around people's feet."

* * *

In a Houston, Texas, court, M—— G—— charged that he couldn't sleep at night because his wife kept a butcher knife under the pillow, and in Cleveland a husband was granted a divorce after telling the court that his wife regularly took $147 out of his weekly $147.50 pay check. Farther West, in Minneapolis, a husband was granted a decree after he found a pair of shorts four times too big for him in his bureau drawer.

* * *

G—— D—— got a divorce because she felt her husband no longer loved her. First, he tried to choke her. Then he made the car skid and tried to hit a pole on her side. Once he threatened to burn down the house after she was in bed. And when she said she was leaving, he offered to pack her bag.

* * *

* * *

DAFFY DIVORCES

A Salt Lake City husband sued for divorce after two years and ten months of marriage, charging that his wife had "failed, neglected and refused to provide the plaintiff with necessities of life."

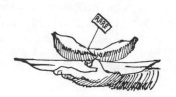

*   *   *

M—— H—— of Oakland, California, received a postcard from her husband reading: "Are you upset? Are you nervous? Do you smoke too much? Try a California divorce for a quick sedative action." That was the remedy she took.

*   *   *

An angry wife in Oregon told the judge that she was willing to forgive her husband for coming home drunk and blackening her eye, but when he asked her the next day how she got the shiner—that was the end.

*   *   *

In a Los Angeles divorce action, one member of the so-called stronger sex brought down the courtroom when he told the judge that, after accusing his wife of infidelity she retorted, "The birds and the bees do it, so I'm going to do it too." Another case involved a deaf-mute who divorced his wife because she nagged him in sign language. A professional wrestler got a divorce because his wife threw him twice in a row.

*   *   *

A judge in Camden, New Jersey, recommended divorce for Mrs. J—— L—— after she testified that her husband kept a revolver and a bullet marked with her initials, and often remarked, "This bullet is especially for you, dear." In Cleveland, a well-known business man complained to the divorce court that every time he forgot to kiss his wife in the morning she fined him $80.

*   *   *

DAFFY DIVORCES

In New Haven, Connecticut, a husband told the court he did not mind working nights in a factory to support his wife and her five

unemployed brothers, but they made so much noise during the day that he could get no sleep.

*　　*　　*

In Detroit, C. A. J. won a divorce after testifying that her husband often came home from a tavern at 4 A.M. and demanded that she put on a one-woman floor show—which lasted "until 9 or 10 o'clock in the morning, or until I got too tired to dance any more."

*　　*　　*

Mrs. G—— G—— thought her husband carried the matter of pets too far. He not only took the dog to bed and kissed it goodnight, but he left the window open for the cat, which used to bring live gophers in and out all night. She got the divorce.

*　　*　　*

In Chicago, Mrs. M—— R—— testified that after a 99-day honeymoon cruise, her husband informed her that since he already had a housekeeper, a chauffeur, and a laundress, he did not need a wife.

*　　*　　*

In Waukesha, Wisconsin, a woman won a divorce from her husband because "he made me nervous getting up at five o'clock every morning to scrub the floors and do the ironing."

* * *

In Chicago, Mrs. H—— L—— got a divorce after testifying she had spoiled her husband's romance with another woman by hiding his toupee. She then generously gave it back to him because "she had no desire to handicap him in his future romantic adventures."

* * *

In a Chicago suit for divorce, a flustered husband complained that his wife not only forbade him to read any magazines with pictures of women in them, but would not allow him to read about women in newspapers and turned off the radio and television whenever a woman was on.

* * *

Mrs. E—— D—— obtained a divorce and eight chickens she and her husband owned jointly after her lawyer explained that she was extremely fond of chickens, "roasted, stewed or fried."

Mrs. E. L. S. brought a divorce action because her husband used her three pet goldfish for bait when he went fishing.

* * *

* * *

DAFFY DIVORCES

A Detroit circuit judge ruled that a wife has the right to go through her husband's pockets, after Mrs. W—— N——, seeking a divorce, testified that her husband tucked his trousers under his mattress every night to keep her away from his money. Mrs. J—— A—— asked for a divorce because her husband would ride in the back seat of their car and reach over to pull her hair and box her ears while she was driving.

* * *

A Baltimore husband filed for divorce on the grounds of desertion after he read a note left behind by his wife, in which she wrote: "Dear F——, don't be so good to your next wife."

A southern California wife gained her freedom when she told the court that while her mouth was wired shut because of a fractured jaw, her husband kept nagging her and she couldn't talk back.

* * *

In Denver, Mrs. E—— K—— angrily testified that her husband wore pajamas at the dinner table when they had guests and often refused to sleep in the bedroom, instead spending the night in the bathtub even though he rarely took a bath.

* * *

* * *

Mrs. M——V——, suing for divorce in Portland, Maine, complained that her husband (a) hung his late first wife's clothes in their bedroom closet, (b) kept an urn of her ashes in the living room, (c) framed her pressed funeral flowers on the wall, and (d) always bought two Christmas trees and explained: "One is for us—the other for her."

* * *

Freak Squeaks

No other single organization in the United States has a more complete record of causes and effects of accidents than the National Safety Council. In the continuing compilation of human error in auto accidents, investigators find that, frequently, the motorist gets an assist from the birds, the bees, animals, children and inanimate objects, which contribute to the unusual, unpredictable, the ludicrous and the laughable, which is what we offer the reader here.

Timothy Davis made headlines in Long Beach, California, by taking his aged grandfather for a spin in the family car. The trip was newsworthy for three reasons. One was that the car tore off the front porch of a nearby house and came so near to running down a neighbor that she fainted. The second was that Timothy propelled the car by sitting on the accelerator. The third was that Timmy was only two years old. Timmy's mother had left him in the car with his grandfather. Timmy turned on the ignition, then sat on the gas pedal, and — *swoosh!*

If a two -year-old boy can drive a car by sitting on the accelerator, a two-year-old girl can do it too — and do it better. Margaret Ann Kilby of Indianapolis was not content to crash in to a mere house. She rammed into a fire-plug, knocked out the neighborhood water supply for three hours, turned the street into a sheet of ice, and, of course, wrecked the car.

*　*　*

Every pedestrian who has lost out to a motorist will admire and applaud the behavior of a hitch-hiking deer in Connecticut. The deer stepped into the road right in front of C—— P—— of Unionville. Startled, Mr. P—— swerved his motorcycle, and the next thing he knew, the deer was seated, somewhat clumsily, on the handlebars. This couldn't last, and a moment later P——, the deer and the motorcycle were sprawled along the roadside. The deer picked itself up, glared balefully at Mr. P—— and with quiet dignity walked over and kicked him in the pants.

*   *   *

Neatest automotive acrobatics of the year were performed by E—— S—— in Philadelphia. His car went out of control on a bridge over the Schuylkill, ripped through the iron bridge railing, turned a complete somersault in the air, and landed on its wheels on a railroad siding 60 feet below, blowing out all four tires. Mr. S—— was dazed, cut up a bit, but, most of all, disappointed. "My tires," he moaned. "Four blowouts in sixty feet. They don't make them like they used to."

*   *   *

S—— B—— of Rochester, New York, eased his auto gently over a railroad crossing to make sure he didn't break two dozen eggs he was taking home. A freight engine bore down on him, struck his car and knocked it into the path of another locomotive on the adjoining track. Mr. B —— crawled from the wreckage to find nothing broken, not even an egg.

*   *   *

R —————— F —————— of Woodland, California, had good reason for momentarily losing his head while driving: a woodpecker was pecking away at it!

The bird, a family pet, was in the lap of F—— 's son when it mistook the elder Fleming's cranium for a tree and went to work. The car left the highway and rolled over twice. Neither of the Flemings was hurt. The woodpecker found itself a tree.

*   *   *

So everything happens to you? Maybe you just think it does. For instance:

Have you ever been shot by your car door? By your dog? By a fish?

Have you swallowed your toothbrush? Has your dog driven your automobile?

Have you proudly named your place Dew Drop Inn only to have it do just that — into the lake?

Gene Scott of Rushville, Nebraska, had hoped his hunting trip would turn up something special. It did. He got shot by his car door. Gene was getting out of the car when a gust of wind blew the door shut on his coat pocket. In the pocket was a rifle shell. Bang!

In New Liberty, Iowa, a twelve-year-old placed his rifle against a ladder in the barn and started to climb to the loft. His dog Terry jumped on the ladder, struck the rifle trigger with his paw, and shot his ascending master just below the hayloft.

Some fish stories are greeted by raised eyebrows. But when Bobby Bright of Gonzales, Texas, reported that he had been shot by a fish, no one could doubt him. He had the fish, the gun and the wound to prove it! A freshly caught catfish flopped around in the bottom of Bobby's boat, struck the trigger of his rifle and shot him in the arm.

Records show that at least two dogs have tried their paws at driving an automobile — a Doberman pinscher in Fort Wayne, Indiana, and a boxer in Black River Falls, Wisconsin. Both ended up by crashing into something. They also ended up in the doghouse.

The Dew Drop Inn at Port Huron, Michigan, lived up to its name during a wild wind- and rain-storm, and dropped into Anchor Bay.

And in Detroit, Mrs. D —— G —— brushed her teeth so vigorously she swallowed the toothbrush.

* * *

Mrs. P—— E —— of Richmond, Indiana, hit a streak of luck when she crashed in to a truck on an icy highway. She was thrown from her car and cozily skidded 200 feet over the ice — on her briefcase.

Eugene Cromwell of Milwaukee wasn't so lucky. Although uninjured when his car swerved off an icy highway, he stepped out to survey the damage, fell into a 50-foot limestone quarry and broke his arm.

* * *

Sleepwalkers have been around for years, but F —— B —— of Fort Lauderdale, Florida, was different — she was a sleepdriver. One night she got out of bed, went to the garage, started the car. The crash which followed woke her with a start and the damages opened her eyes even more — $450 to the garage and $300 to the car.

* * *

J—— D—— of Oklahoma City was turning a corner when the steering mechanism of his car went haywire. The car climbed a telephone pole guy-wire, flipped through some trees and crashed to the ground upside down. The only injury Davis suffered was a lump on the head — caused when he released his seat belt and dropped onto the car roof.

* * *

FREAK SQUEAKS

F—— and G—— W——, of Little Rock, Arkansas, met on the highway — head on. The first thing each driver did was to rush to the other car and display regret over the damage. They weren't just being noble. An hour earlier they had swapped cars for the day.

* * *

James Palmer of Akron and James Fox of Kent, Ohio, tell one of the most incredible fish stories ever heard. Returning at nightfall after a day's fishing, they were startled when a big muskie flopped into their boat. It swatted Fox in the face with its tail and broke Palmer's fishing rod, then flipped out of the boat and swam off.

* * *

Do you think feminine curiosity is overrated? Well, in Pasadena, Mrs. E —— K —— arrived at a railroad crossing to find the wigwags wigwagging full tilt. Intrigued, she drove on the tracks to see what was coming. It was a train, of all things. She backed up hastily, but the locomotive caught the front bumper of her car. Mrs. K ——, her curiosity satisfied, was unhurt.

* * *

No one was injured when four cars piled up in a collision near Des Moines. No one, that is, until Patrolman E—— V——, investigating the crash, slammed a car door on his finger.

And in Santa Monica, California, police arrested a motorist for the second time in 18 months. His name? — Safety First.

In Redlands, California, a driver named — believe it or not — Mr. O. Bee Good was advised by police to live up to his name after they had apprehended him running a stop light and colliding with a truck.

*   *   *

Hauled into court when his car crashed into another, J —— S —— of Logansport, Indiana, admitted he had been suffering from a hangover. "But it was an ice cream hangover, Your Honor," he told the judge. "I ate so much ice cream that I cut loose with a big burp and lost control of my car."

*   *   *

Four-year-old Walter Adams Jr. was showing his younger brother some acrobatic stunts he had seen on TV when he happened to glance out the window of his fourth-floor apartment in New York City. He noticed that several small girls on the sidewalk forty feet below were observing his antics. Walter decided to show them something really good. He opened the window, put his hands together like a high diver, and took off. The girls pulled him out of a big snowbank and carried him up, crying, to his mother. Nothing was hurt but his pride.

*   *   *

The sign over the door of a used-car salesroom in Los Angeles read: "We need your car — drive in." L —— J —— did just that — with his throttle stuck. The car crashed through a heavy wooden door, sideswiped two glistening cars on the salesroom floor, ran head-on into a costly convertible and bounced it into another car. They took down the sign.

* * *

Mrs. L —— L —— is used to hearing her neighbors in Cedar Rapids, Iowa, say that her biscuits are always sure-fire. Nonetheless, she was startled when shots rang out from the hot oven into which she had just popped a pan of dough. Then she remembered that when the family left on a recent vacation, two revolvers had been hidden in the stove.

* * *

In 1956, two-year-old Jeffrey McGuire should have been the dryest boy in Cleveland — but he wasn't, because of his tears. That was the day he crawled into the family laundry dryer and his young brother obligingly pulled the switch. Mrs. McGuire, making the usual rounds to see what her sons were up to, found and rescued Jeff in the nick of time.

* * *

On a highway near Meridian, Mississippi, Mrs. G. D. Middleton saw something fall from a station wagon traveling ahead of her. She picked it up, figured the people in the station wagon would eventually miss it and want it back, and took off to overtake them. She had a time doing it, too, for the couple in the station wagon thought the pursuing driver just wanted to play games. Mrs. Middleton finally caught up, after a 15-mile chase, and returned the lost object. And was the couple in the station wagon ever glad to get it back, practically undamaged. It was their two-year-old son.

*   *   *

No man who has ever struggled into a dress shirt will be too surprised at what happened to John H. Bradford of Richmond, Virginia. As director of the state budget, Mr. Bradford had pulled out of some mighty tight squeezes — but none as tight as the collar he tried to button one night in dolling himself up for an important party. Director Bradford fought so fiercely that he had to go to the hospital for emergency treatment of severe finger bruises inflicted by the collar button.

*   *   *

Even more embarrassing was the experience of Officer D —— O —— of Detroit. As the young policeman was strolling with his girl-friend on his night off, his service pistol let go and shot off the seat of his pants.

The celebrated case of the cantankerous cockroach occured in Detroit and involved John Nantico, a bakery employee. Mr. Nantico said he was ascending stairs made slippery by spilled cake frosting when he looked into the leering eyes of the biggest cockroach any man ever saw. Mr. Nantico aimed a knockout kick at the roach with his right foot. The roach ducked. Mr. Nantico's left and anchor foot slipped in the frosting and he hurtled end over end to the floor below. His kicking leg was broken.

*　　*　　*

"Knowing how to fall and jump is very important," Con Dempsey, former Pittsburgh Pirate pitcher, told his junior high school physical education class in San Francisco. With this observation he stepped briskly back, tripped over a mat, fell flat and broke his arm.

*　　*　　*

100

In Cincinnati youthful Judy Combs devised a system for getting down stairs that not only is faster than an escalator, but more exciting. Judy rolled off a fourth-floor fire escape, fell twenty feet, landed on a network of clothes-lines and bounced back onto the fire escape on the second floor of her apartment building. She didn't even cry.

*   *   *

It was hard for young M ——— F ——— to figure out just how he happened to ram his bike in to a parked car on a street in Miami Beach. "All I was doing," he told the police, "was riding along reading my comic book."

*   *   *

In 1950 Mickey Holloway of Birmingham, Alabama, was as pleased as any two-year-old boy would be at his fascinating ability to make faces at his older sister. The faces were even more satisfactory, Mickey discovered, when they were framed between the bars of the bannister in his home. You guessed it: his head got caught between the bars. Firemen pried him loose. Even his sister felt sorry for him — a little.

But the boy who emerged head and shoulders above any other head-sticker-into of 1950 was young Philip Burrows. Phil also was only two years old, but he had the advantage of living in Hollywood, California, where they do things more spectacularly. So Phil chose to steal headline honors by getting his head stuck in, of all things, a toilet seat. Even the firemen, accustomed to this kind of crisis, were impressed as they went to work with a saw to dethrone him.

* * *

A Dallas housewife, Mrs. E.L.C., investigated a noise in the bedroom, reported back to her husband, "Honey, there's a car in your bed."

There was, too. The auto had missed a turn in a skyscraper parking garage next to the hotel where the C ———s lived, leaped six feet through space and crashed through the wall of their third-floor bedroom. No one was injured, but Mr. C ——— made the car get out.

* * *

Fully aware that things are tough all over, police in Sacramento nevertheless were surprised to get a report that an automobile had picked the pocket of a pedestrian and escaped with $102. The victim had walked too close to a moving car. His coat pocket — wallet and all — was ripped off by the auto and carried away.

* * *

G ——— B ———, a Southern Illinois University coed, had some difficulty studying after her uncle got thirsty. He saw G ——— with a glass of water, reached for it, and gulped it down before she could stop him. Her contact lenses were soaking in the water with which Uncle slaked his thirst.

*   *   *

And in Knoxville, Tennessee, G ——— G ——— reached absent-mindedly for a cigarette, stuck a two-inch firecracker into his mouth and lit it. From his hospital bed he announced he had given up smoking.

*   *   *

And in Fort Worth, W.L. Daniel Jr. was listening intently to a talk on safety in an aircraft plant. Displayed proudly on the wall above him was a hard-won safety plaque. Suddenly everything went black for Mr. Daniel. The safety plaque had fallen and bopped him on the head.

*   *   *

Have you ever had anyone almost talk an arm off you? Mrs. J ——— A ——— of Memphis almost did it to herself. Chatting animatedly to a friend over the phone, she flung an arm in an emphatic gesture, hit the corner of a desk, and broke a bone.

*   *   *

Each year at least one field mouse leaves the field to get into an automobile and cause an accident. Recently, a roving rodent hitched a ride in a car driven by F—— J—— of St. Louis. It was discovered by Mrs. J——, who did just what came naturally. Her startled husband drove off the road and banged into a hydrant. The lady went to the doctor. The car went to the garage. The field mouse went back to the field.

*   *   *

Possibly stung by the high cost of living, bees apparently quit riding in private automobiles and democratically took to streetcars. A merry group of them informally boarded a trolley in Cincinnati through an open window and evinced high interest in the motorman. As he frantically batted at his bumbling passengers, the streetcar bumped an auto, which rammed the rear of another, which rammed the rear of another.

*   *   *

In Cincinnati, C—— B——'s car was struck by two trains traveling in opposite directions. He was left standing on the tracks, steering wheel in hand, suffering only from cuts and bruises, complicated by acute amazement.

*   *   *

FREAK SQUEAKS

The J—— B——s of Bellflower, California, didn't have to lift a hand to arrange for a rumpus with which to christen their new rumpus room. A passing automobile obliged by going out of control and crashing into the room for one of the biggest rumpuses ever put on.

* * *

Then there are the traffic experts who say it's safe to go through a green light. Try and tell that to motorist E. T. D. of Atlanta, Georgia. As Mr. D—— obeyed an overhead traffic light that flashed a green go-ahead signal, the light crashed down on top of his car and sent him to the hospital.

* * *

Oddities in the News

Strange things happen every day to Americans in every walk of life. Some of the happenings are reported as straight news, others are reflected in the public notices and classified ads on the back pages.

In Richmond, Indiana, a twelve-year-old visitor from the country carefully explained why he had turned in a false fire alarm: Some city boys had told him that if he pulled the lever in the red box, a bird would pop out and forecast the weather.

*   *   *

In Tyler, Texas, sportscaster Ed Smith announced during a baseball game that someone had left his car lights on in the parking lot, repeatedly gave the car's description and license number, remembered at game's end that it was his.

*   *   *

In Buffalo, New York, the Board of Supervisors got a letter from a county resident protesting payment of a $9 sales tax on a funeral bill: "I think it is an outrage . . . I know St. Peter won't like it."

*   *   *

A judge in St. Louis was taken aback when a woman witness refused to answer the first, and completely routine, question "on the grounds that it might incriminate me." Surprised — the woman was a witness for the State — the judge asked her if her lawyer had advised her to refuse. "Oh, no, Your Honor," she replied, "I learned that on television."

* * *

In Sioux Falls, South Dakota, the house shook with laughter when C —— S ——, local featherweight, took off his robe for his Golden Gloves boxing match: he had forgotten to wear his boxing trunks into the ring. The match was held up while he returned to the dressing room. He lost the bout, but won the sportsmanship trophy.

In Indianapolis, reporter Bruce Hilton stood on the street with dark glasses, guitar, a tin cup, and a sign announcing: "I am not blind, deaf, dumb or crippled, and do not want any money," in 40 minutes collected 29 cents.

* * *

After running for mayor of Ripley, Tennessee, and getting only 57 out of 1,163 votes cast, Dr. J —— F —— announced that he would contest the election, demand a recount: "I have more than 57 relatives . . . who I know voted for me."

* * *

A farmer in Gadsden, Alabama, explained to the judge why he did not send his two children, aged nine and eleven, to school: "They both take snuff, and there is no place in the classroom to spit."

*   *   *

From a North Dakota paper: "Will trade girl's coat, age 7, or pair of women's oxfords, size 2, or copy of Woman and the New Race by Margaret Sanger, for five yards of gingham."

*   *   *

When a jittery woman passenger screamed every time a Toledo, Ohio, bus came to a halt, driver Emil Jefferson finally stopped the bus for good, told her: "You make me nervous. I quit."

*   *   *

In Chicago two gunmen invaded the home of L ——— F ———, discovered that he was away, entertained the baby-sitter and Mr. F ———'s children with fairy tales until he returned, then robbed him of $4,525 in cash and an estimated $7,000 in jewelry.

*   *   *

The Des Moines, Iowa park board disallowed night watchman A ——— W ———'s claim for new false teeth because, when the baseball thrown during an amateur game broke his set, his dentures were in his pocket.

*   *   *

From the Salt Lake City Tribune: "NOTICE to our friends, to bill collectors, radio and TV poll takers, et al: Due to our daughter's return from college for the holidays, we expect a 30-minute to three-hour delay on all telephone calls to our residence. Mr. and Mrs. H.H.F."

*   *   *

From the DeKalb [Illinois] Daily Chronicle: "Day Nursery — Expert supervision for ages six weeks to five years. By hour or day. Unreasonable rates for unreasonable children."

*   *   *

In Paul Valley, Oklahoma, H ——— H ——— was charged with grand larceny in the theft of a $50 outhouse.

*   *   *

ODDITIES IN THE NEWS

From the Elberton [Georgia] Star: "Notice. This is to certify that I know the forked-tongued, snake-eyed skunk that killed my Doberman pinscher dog in cold blood. I certainly know the 'Judy Hole' in the Savannah River where he took a rock and tied it to him and sank him in twenty feet of water to keep the buzzards away so that I could not find him. If the man will have the nerve to come to me and admit it, I will give him $10 provided he will be able to put it in his pocket when I get through with him."

* * *

Appearing in a New York paper on succeeding days: "Avery — Time growing short. Am getting desperate. Must meet you to obtain your information on what a durwood kirby is. Aunt Aggie."

"Aunt Aggie — Getting warm. Should have something new to report on a durwood kirby soon. Contact me in this column again regarding next meeting. Avery."

* * *

R —— B —— of Washington, D.C., was fined $10 for holding hands with a girl: He was driving one car; she was riding in another.

* * *

In Hobbs, New Mexico, Fire Chief Archie Conner shut down his department for two days, posted a warning: "Positively no fires allowed."

* * *

In the San Antonio [Texas] Light: "$10 REWARD to anyone giving name and address of party that removed three-room frame house and barn in rear of 113 North Pecos Street . . ."

* * *

In a Connecticut newspaper on March 22: "Slightly used warm wench in good condition, Very handy. Phone 000-R-2. A —— C ——."

———

Ditto, March 29: "Correction. Due to an unfortunate error, Mr. C ——'s ad last week was not clear. He has an excellent winch for sale. We trust this will put an end to jokesters who have called Mr. C —— and greatly bothered his housekeeper, Mrs. H ——, who loves him."

———

Ditto, April 5: "NOTICE! My WINCH is not for sale. I put a sledgehammer to it. Don't bother calling 000-R-2. I had the phone taken out. I am NOT carrying on with Mrs. H ——. She merely LIVES here. A —— C ——."

* * *

In Salina, Kansas, a prowler stole $20 worth of fishing poles and reels from Claude W. Peters's garage, then borrowed a spade and dug for worms in Peters's back yard.

A Tulsa motorist explained to the court why he had smashed into a car driven by a woman ahead of him: "She signaled she was going to turn right, and then she turned right."

* * *

From the Galena Park [Texas] Channel Press: "Emma — Come on home. All forgiven. My upper plate is still in your purse."

* * *

114

ODDITIES IN THE NEWS

In the Duluth News-Tribune: "As far as my husband, M —— S ——, not being responsible for my bills, he never was. I have always paid the bills as he usually doesn't work. L —— A —— S ——."

*   *   *

In a Western daily paper: If J.C., who 22 years ago basely deserted his helpless, penniless wife and son, Michael, will return home, Mike will take pleasure in knocking hell out of him.

*   *   *

In Indianapolis store clerk H —— A —— was robbed three times in two weeks by the same man, protested: "He walks in here like he owned the place."

In San Francisco a stranger stabbed Lawrence Bridges in the neck, knocked him to the sidewalk, then said: "Pardon me, I thought you were Jerry."

*   *   *

*   *   *

In the Casey County [Kentucky] News: "To the person who is so destitute as to be forced to take two lengths of garden hose and a sprinkler from the lawn of the First Christian Church — if you will call at the pastor's study, he will give you the five-year guarantee for the hose, your dinner, and any religion that may rub off on you."

*   *   *

ODDITIES IN THE NEWS

In Youngstown, Ohio, G—— O——, 24, ignored the railroad brakeman's red lantern, drove on until she crashed into a train, later explained: "I didn't want to stop in the neighborhood after dark."

* * *

In Meriden, Connecticut, a woman driver got a parking ticket. "But, Officer," she said, "I was trying on a girdle and they gave me a size too small. I couldn't get out of it in time to put in a second nickel." The ticket cost her $1 anyway.

* * *

In Chicago, Mrs. V—— F—— gave birth to a baby girl in a taxicab on the way to the hospital, said she had phoned for the cab instead of waking up her cab-driver husband because "he works at night, and I hated to disturb him."

* * *

In Nashville, Tennessee, a jewelry store operator figured a sale of coffee for 49 cents a pound would bring customers into his store. The

In Toledo, Ohio, the public library got back a copy of *David Crockett: His Life and Adventures* borrowed in 1882, decided that the best thing to do was just forget about the fine of $788.

* * *

In Oskaloosa, Iowa, L—— M——, 62, protested that his dog Queenie actually was at the wheel when he was arrested for drunken driving. Authorities, however, jailed him in lieu of $1,000 bond and let Queenie go free.

* * *

customers came, bought 1,600 pounds of coffee—at a net loss to the operator of $656: none bought any jewelry.

* * *

ODDITIES IN THE NEWS

In Ithaca, New York, E—— J——, meteorologist at the U.S. Weather Bureau office in Albany, apologized for arriving late at a speaking engagement, said his plane had been held up by unexpected weather.

*   *   *

Near Peru, Indiana, C—— W—— was arrested for drunken driving after he mistook the Chesapeake & Ohio RR tracks for the road to his home, forced an oncoming train to stop, then bawled out the engineer for not dimming his lights.

In Houston, Texas, W. D. T., hospitalized after a fight in which he suffered two black eyes and a broken leg, was asked if he wanted to prefer charges against his assailant, told police: "No, he's a friend of mine."

*   *   *

In the Phoenix (Arizona) Republic's "Lost" column: "Teeth, uppers near Avalon on South Central; lowers near Riverside ballroom . . ."

*   *   *

In a New York City paper: The woman I want should be married and have children, but not necessarily. I want a woman who can bake excellent pies. I'll buy the ingredients per your specifications. You use my kitchen right here in New York. Five days a week. I'll pay your salary. You name it.

*   *   *

In Cincinnati, Ohio, a bandit held up T—— K——, relieved him of $26, handed him a quarter and advised: "Take a bus home."

*   *   *

*   *   *

ODDITIES IN THE NEWS

In Detroit, soon after a passenger announced "this is a stickup" and told him to "keep on going," Cab Driver A—— S—— noticed that his fare had dozed off, kept on going to the police station.

* * *

In Jal, New Mexico, after police had put up a traffic sign reading: "School Zone—Don't Kill a Child,"

It pays to advertise, C—— K——, of Nebraska City, Nebraska, agrees. Someone stole his overcoat and he inserted this ad in the *Nebraska City News-Press:* "I wish a Merry Christmas to the person who stole my coat." The next day he got his coat in the mail.

* * *

In a North Dakota daily: Wanted immediately—unfurnished apartment or house: man, wife and daughter, 8, and dog. Will dispose of dog, but prefer to keep child.

* * *

they found a postscript written in a childish scrawl: "Wait for a Teacher."

* * *

Fort Worth (Texas) Press: If the lady whose girdle I wore away by mistake calls 6-3354 I will gladly exchange.

* * *　　　　* * *

118

ODDITIES IN THE NEWS

In New Orleans, Seaman E—— M—— was arrested after he walked into a dime store, freed four canaries and nine parakeets from their cages, saying: "Come on out—I was in jail once. I know how you feel."

* * *

In San Fernando, California, J—— C—— got a gift-wrapped, four-foot boa constrictor from her boy friend, who explained: "I wanted to give her something different."

In the Bennington, Vermont, Banner: Young business girl would like another girl to share her furnished apartment. Must squeeze toothpaste from the bottom.

* * *   * * *

A Connecticut newspaper: Liz— Thought you would like to know I've been on the wagon for two months. T.

———

Joe—There has been a man in the neighborhood seeking information about you. I think he's a bill collector. Mom.

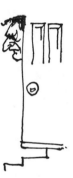

* * *

Abilene, Texas: $10 reward for south-side apartment. Large enough to keep young wife from going home to mother, small enough to keep mother from coming here.

In a Larchmont, New York, paper: Tombstone for sale with the name of "John Murphy" carved on it. Stone contracted for in 1937 and uncalled for.

* * *   * * *

ODDITIES IN THE NEWS

Apartment hunting in Fresno, California, is really wacky, as witness this ad from the *Fresno Bee:* Half-wit vet, 3 dogs, 4 cats, a chronic alcoholic, wife and small monster on the way, desires a small apt. to practice his homework. Majoring [Fresno State College] in house-wrecking, intends to take up drums.

* * *

In the Palestine (Texas) Herald: Your dog ain't getting much out of my garbage pail, so why don't you feed him.

* * *

The Princeton (West Virginia) Observer: I will pay $5 reward to any party who will admit to my wife that he threw the whiskey bottles in my garden.

* * *

In the Austin (Texas) Tribune: Notice to car thieves: My tires are puncture-proof. If you try to steal them, you had better be puncture-proof too.

* * *

Chattanooga (Tennessee) Times: Restaurant business for sale. Need money for Orange Bowl game.

* * *

The Boston Herald: Hearse. 1937 La Salle. Not a scratch on it. Best thing in the world for a skiing trip.

* * *

The Publishers' Auxiliary on January 1, 1943, carried this classified gem under "Help Wanted, Editorial": Girl journalism graduate with at least a year's weekly experience on news and ads needed badly to assist publisher of good weekly. Prefer girl who is perfect 36, beautiful, smart, willing to work for $5 a week, interested in weekly papers, Protestant, Catholic, Jewish, white or colored. Because of war we might waive some or all preferences. Office is cold in winter, hot as hell in summer,

the toughest weekly joint in the state to work in because we're ornery. We also expect perfection in other folks. We serve beer when the 40-year-old press has a birthday and serve sarcastic remarks anytime. You'll suffer here, but you'll be a newspaper man or fired before you go, so don't come for a two-month holiday. We just finished making a swell newspaper man out of a guy with a Wisconsin M.A., but right now he wants to sleep in Navy hammocks. Of course, if can cook, too, or use a speed graphic it wouldn't hurt, but you don't have to sweep the floors or wash windows or melt metal. If you want to take a chance, tell us something about yourself and what you read and what your plans are. If you've got questions, ask 'em. We don't want you here only two weeks any more than you want to get fired or quit. We've got the swellest staff in the state, or did have until the war, and we want to keep half-way good. (Oh yes, don't worry. My wife can cook good.) G. W. G., *Leader News,* Waupum, Wisconsin.

*   *   *

Los Angeles Westchester Airport Tribune: Young lady with 1941 Chevrolet desires to meet personable young man mechanically inclined.

* * *

An ad in Daily Variety: I surrender. Young man with no agent, no contract, no roles, will give up promising career as actor for interesting job.

* * *

In the Miami (Florida) Herald: Ann. Heart condition made me make a solemn promise to obey all the commandments of God. I cannot see you again. Zeke

* * *

A moving and storage company in Chicago placed the following classified ad in a Chicago newspaper: Our help are all tired—so unless you need anything real bad, do not come this week.

* * *

ODDITIES IN THE NEWS

A furniture store in Janesville, Wisconsin, advertised: "Will the mother whose little boy laid his sucker on an end table come in? She can have the end table for just $1, with sucker still intact."

* * *

St. Peter (Minnesota) Herald: WANTED: Man to handle dynamite. Must be prepared to travel unexpectedly.

* * *

The McLeansboro (Illinois) Times-Leader: Will the person or persons who took all my hens and left the old rooster come and get him. He is lonesome.

* * *

Eagle Pass (Texas) News Guide: WANTED AT ONCE—Am desperate account of continued livestock thefts. Need watchman that can shoot. Will pay by hour or by head.

* * *

123